THE FIRST SPITFIRE

1. Dani Shapira boarding Spitfire "white 12" at Azion air strip, north of the Negev, in 1949 (see page39). (Dani Shapira)

With Israel's War Of Independence placing enormous demands on its fledgling Air Force, the need for fighter aircraft was desperate. Efforts, up until the early stage of the war, had concentrated on scouring the world to purchase suitable aircraft and rushing them to Israel by any means necessary.

In May 1948, negotiations with the Czechoslovakian government resulted in the acquisition of 25 Avia S-199 fighters and talks began regarding the purchase of Czech Spitfire Mk IXs. However, the first Spitfires to actually enter the Israeli Air Force (IAF) inventory were two Mk IXs assembled from abandoned British and captured Egyptian airframes.

As Britain's Mandate to control Palestine expired and the State of Israel came into existence on 15 May 1948, the Royal Air Force (RAF) withdrew from its bases there and left behind a rich cache of aircraft wrecks in dumps adjacent to it's old air bases. One

such dump was at Ein Shemer in northern Israel, formerly home to 32 and 208 Squadrons, where IAF technicians recovered three Spitfire Mk IX fuselages and a large quantity of spare parts. This collection of matériel was initially worked on in Tel Aviv and later Ma'arbarot, north of the City. One of the fuselages came from 208 Sqn's 'RG-W' which had been field modified for photo-reconnaissance purposes and most likely formed the basis of D-130, the first IAF Spitfire. D-130's wings and engine were scavenged from a Royal Egyptian Air Force (REAF) Spitfire Mk IX,

shot down over Sde Dov, by anti-aircraft fire, on 15 May 1948. D-130 was completed and put through taxiing trials and by late August /early September 1948 the technicians were ready to hand it over to 101 Squadron.

Boris Senior came to Ma'arbarot to make D-130s first true test flight, which doubled as it's delivery flight to 101 Sqn at Herzliyya. The author has interviewed Senior several times but he could not recall the exact date of this first flight, or confirm it from his log books, as these had been stolen from his private Beech Bonanza while in Europe years later.

Within weeks Spitfire D-131, the second IAF Spitfire, was also in the air. Its ex RAF fuselage was combined with the wings and engine recovered from an Egyptian Spitfire shot down by the RAF over Ramat David on 22 May 1948.

The new Spitfires were a tremendous boost to 101 Squadron in the air superiority role. Initially neither was fitted out for ground-attack work to support the army and in any case, within a month, D-130 was reconfigured for photo-reconnaissance duties (including one such flight over Damascus in mid November 1948) with the installation of a single belly camera. It was stripped back to bare metal, had its armament removed and was given full 101

Squadron markings including the now famous "Angel Of Death" badge on the port nose. D-130, now designated 2001, eventually suffered an electrical fire at Ramat David in 1951 and was written-off.

D-131 became 2002 "White 11", also with full 101 Sqn markings. There is an element of doubt about D-131's new serial although both D-131 and 2002 had the same style of nonstandard rear-view mirror (taken from a car!), no underwing racks, the same type of wing-tips and early style rudder. 2002 survived until the Spitfire went out of IAF service in April 1956.

There are Indications that a third Spitfire was built from recovered RAF parts in 1949, although proof has never been established (see page 8).

Photos 2 3 & 4. - taken on the same day at Ma'arbarot air strip, July/August 1948

D-130 was painted in dark green primer at this stage with no national insignia. The technicians chalked it with the name "Israel 1", it's serial number, their names and various inscriptions in English and Hebrew. During this period at Ma'arbarot only taxiing trials and short 'hops' were made, with no actual flights being risked because of persistent engine overheating. This was the last problem to be overcome before handing D-130 over to 101 Squadron.

2. A group of technicians act as ballast while Maurice Mann taxies D-130. Note the faired-over camera port still in bare metal. (Yuda Borowick)

3. Maurice Mann beside D-130. Of great interest is the chalked on Donald Duck cartoon head, a good indication of the influence of former USAAF/USN pilots at this formative stage of the IAF. (Author)

4. The same group of technicians pose for the camera in front of D-130. Note the unpainted radio mast and cannon bay panel, no yellow prop tips and heavily scuffed wing root. The aircraft was being worked on continuously and by the time it was delivered to 101 Squadron other new parts had been added and it's colour scheme included hand painted 'Shield of David' national insignia (SoD). (Yuda Borowick)

Spitfire Mk IX 'RG-W' served with 208 Squadron RAF in 1945 and is thought to have formed the basis of the IAF's D-130.

Its colour scheme was standard *Ocean Grey & Dark Green* upper surfaces with *Medium Sea Grey* under surfaces, sky rear fuselage band, white codes and black spinner. This aircraft was flown by 208's Squadron Leader and carried his pennant in an unusual position behind the cockpit.

Note that the serial number PV120 is provisional.

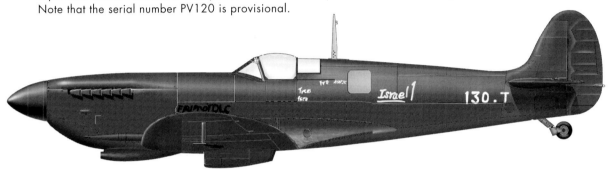

Spitfire Mk IX D-130, following its rebuild at Ma'arbarot, Israel, July/August 1948.

It's colour scheme was a patchy dark green primer with some panels bare metal. White chalk had been used to apply most of the inscriptions, including 'D-130', although much darker wording is visible above the wing root.

Colour renderings of these illustrations appear on the back cover.

5. The RAF aircraft dump at Ein Shemer, near Haifa, in June/July 1948. This Spitfire Mk IX, 'RG-W' of 208 Sqn, had been field-modified for photo-reconnaissance purposes. 'RG-W's fuselage probably formed the basis of D-130.

Standing on the wreck are five IAF technicians who undertook the rebuild.

Literally seconds after this photo was taken Iraqi troops mortared the dump, forcing its temporary evacuation. Following this unwanted distraction, three Spitfire fuselages, plus a large selection of spare parts were salvaged and taken to Tel Aviv where the task of rebuilding them into D-130 and D-131 began. (IAF Archive)

6, 6a & 7. D-130 either about to leave Ma'arbarot or upon arrival at Herzliyya the day it was delivered to 101 Squadron. That day the ground staff performed a long engine test to confirm persistent overheating problems had been cured and handed D-130 over to Boris Senior. He flew two or three short take off and landing circuits then set out for Herzliyya.

Before departure a motorcycle messenger was dispatched to warn 101 Squadron that the first IAF Spitfire would soon be arriving and not to shoot it down!

By this stage large hand-painted SoD have been applied to the fuselage and under wings.

Note the bare metal cannon panel, yellow prop tips, bare metal and RAF camouflaged nose panels and blue spinner. Note too, how roughly painted the white/blue/white rear fuselage ID bands are - *speed was of the essence!* (Yuda Borowick)

In (6 & 6a) Ezer Weisman is standing at the wing root.

7. Boris Senior in the cockpit of D-130 wearing a Luftwaffe style flying helmet. (Author)
Inset, D-130 landing at Herzliyya. (Arnie Ruch)

8. Boris Senior stands in front of D-130. He was one of the first pilots in 101 Sqn and later served at IAF HQ in Tel Aviv. He continued to fly Spitfires during the War of Independence, shooting down an Egyptian Spitfire.

He returned to his native South Africa after the war, but emigrated back to Israel in the 1960s, where he now lives in retirement. (Author)

9. Rudi Augarten warms up D-131 at Herzliyya, Sept/Oct 1948. Underwing SoDs have been applied, along with white/ blue/white rear fuselage identification bands. Of all the IAF Spitfires only D-130 and D-131 ever carried ID bands in this position.

Note the nonstandard rear-view mirror, which was taken from a car, and the red spinner with white backing plate. (Author)

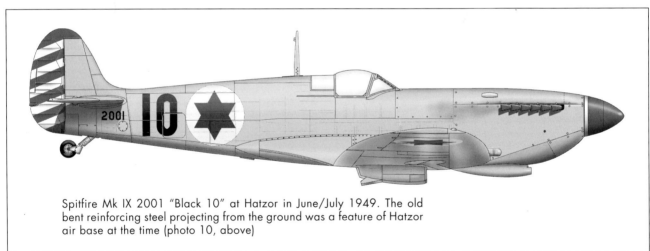

Spitfire Mk IX 2001 "Black 10" at Hatzor in June/July 1949. The old bent reinforcing steel projecting from the ground was a feature of Hatzor air base at the time (photo 10, above)

10(above), **11**(right) **&** **12**(facing page). By October 1948 D-130 had been re-serialed 2001 and given the radio number "Black 10". All paint was removed and new, smaller, standard sized SoD. were applied further back on the fuselage. The 101 Sqn "Angel of Death" badge was retained and red & white rudder stripes added. Just visible under the tailplane in Photo 11 is the 10cm (4 inch) high serial number.

"Black 10" was used solely for reconnaissance duties and had no guns or bomb racks. An anti-glare panel was applied later in it's career.

All three photos were taken during June/July 1949 at Hatzor (also see photo 84). (IDF Archive 10, 12 & Yuda Borowick 11,)

12. "Black 10" in June/July 1949 at Hatzor.

13. Spitfire Mk IX 2002 "White 11", 'buzzes' a United Nations C-47 carrying pilgrims to Mecca, over the Mediterranean near the Gaza Strip, in mid 1949. The white rudder with no red stripes is most unusual. Note the white/blue/white fuselage ID bands and the much smaller blue star portion of the fuselage SoD compared with "Black 10". (Author)

14. Nathan Suffin, of the IAF Aerial Photography Unit, loads a modified British 14" F24 camera into "Black 10" at Hatzor in mid 1949. (via Author)

Two standard WWII F 24 cameras as carried by RAF Spitfires. 14" and 8" lenses are fitted respectively. (via Malcolm Laird)

15. Israeli researchers commonly believe that a third RAF airframe recovered from Ein Shemer was rebuilt in 1949 using additional spares purchased along with the ex-CzAF Spitfires. However, proof of this has never been found.

Perhaps this intriguing photo taken at Hatzor in mid 1949 provides the missing link; on the original print an RAF C-type roundel is more clearly visible under the port wing. This aircraft was not a 'Velveta' machine and can't be either of the two known rebuilds as it had a broad chord rudder and it's fuselage was bare metal at a time when D-130 and D-131, by now "black 10" and "White 11" were well documented in service. Note the wings "C" armament layout, with guns yet to be installed. (IDF Archive)

The badge of 101 Squadron IAF in 1948. It's design has various detail differences to that used today.

16. 101 Sqn pilots use their hands as aircraft while discussing fighter tactics, as pilots have done down through the years. The group are standing in front of "Black 10" at Ramat David, after the squadron moved there from Hatzor in late 1949. By the time this photo was taken a black anti-glare panel had been applied and was already severely faded due to the bright Mediterranean sun.

From the left are Dani Shapira, Joe Cohen, Sam Feldman, Grisha Braun, and Eli Feingash. (Author)

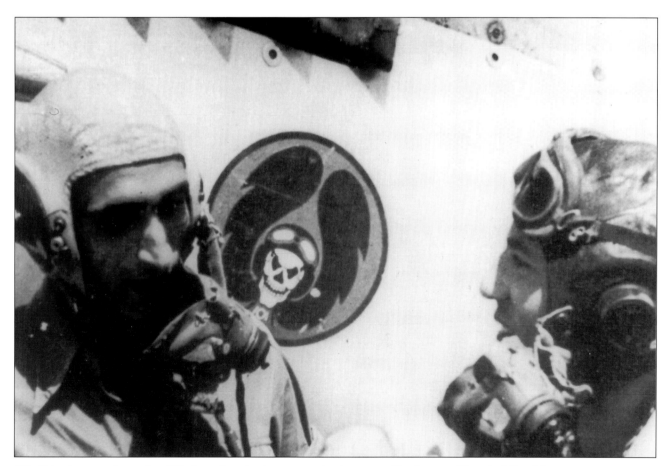

17. This close-up shows the 101 Squadron badge to good advantage. The famous "Angel of Death" badge was designed by 101 Sqn pilot Stan Andrews, an American volunteer, who was shot down and killed on 20 October 1948. It was designed one night in a popular Tel Aviv bar where pilots would meet, discuss the days events and try to relax. It was a lively session that night with the discussion swinging between choosing the 'Angel' or the 'Scorpion' suggested by Modi Alon. The latter eventually became the badge of 105 Squadron in 1950. (Author)

THE CZECH SPITFIRES

18. JT-10 of the 4th Fighter Regiment, CzAF in 1946. (Jaromir Stepan)

Apart from D-130 and D-131 all the Spitfires recorded in this volume are ex-Czechoslovakian Air Force (CzAF). When the Soviet backed communist regime came to power in 1948 they decreed that western aircraft should be dropped from the CzAF inventory and this precipitated the sale of Spitfires to Israel, for much needed hard currency.

Secret negotiations between Czech and Israeli government agencies saw agreement on terms of sale that included aircraft, spares and pilot training. The 1948 sale comprised two batches of 50 & 9 aircraft respectively at a unit price of US$23,000. The Israelis considered this a good price, all things considered and aircraft selection and preparation to export the Spitfires began in June. Two pilot training courses (now known as the "Minus 2" and "Minus 1" courses because they preceded the IAF's first official training courses in Israel) were run with George Lichter and Caesar Dangott acting as Chief Instructors. CzAF staff were also fully involved as instructors.

Part of the fascination of the Israeli Spitfire story, especially for the colours and markings enthusiast, is that as these aircraft passed from British to Czech to Israeli hands, the latter two owners rarely repainted an entire airframe, so that each Spitfire wears its history as a painted patchwork.

19 & 20. Two photos of 3rd Air Division CzAF Spitfires at an air show in Brno-Slatina on 13 October 1946.
IV-9 is PL250 and the only known example of a CzAF Spitfire with the early style rudder. The second photo, framed by the wing of a Ju 52, includes IV-10 SL630. The Division's eagle emblem is clearly visible on the nose. (Jaromir Stepan)

21. Spitfire Mk IX TE554, 'A-708' in 1948 while serving with the CzAF Training Academy. TE554 served with 310 Sqn RAF and then the 10th Fighter Regiment, 1st Air Division, based in Prague. In Israeli service TE554 eventually became the famous "Black Spitfire" flown by Ezer Weisman in the '60s and is now preserved by the IAF Museum. (Jaromir Stepan)

22. JT coded Spitfires of the 4th Fighter Regiment, 2nd Air Division, CzAF. The change-over date from RAF to CzAF was 30 August 1945, with the old RAF codes and Squadron numbers being replaced by those of the new Fighter Regiments (JT etc) on 15 February 1946. The CzAF simply re-camouflaged areas where its own insignia was to be applied.
Note the darker, freshly painted areas on all these aircraft. (Jaromir Stepan)

OPERATION VELVETA

Velveta was the code name given to the operation involving the ferrying by air of some of the fifty nine Czech Spitfire Mk IX's purchased by Israel. A total of 18 set out on the two ferry missions from Czechoslovakia, via Yugoslavia, to Israel between September and December 1948. These flights were attempted purely because of Israel's desperate need for even a few more fighters as her confrontation with neighbouring Arab countries reached crisis point. The code name Velveta covered only the aircraft that were *flown* back to Israel, not the crated and shipped majority. Interestingly, the name 'Velveta' was derived from the brand name of the sunscreen lotion ('Velvetta'

with two 't's) in IAF survival kits of the day.

Even though the IAF was not enamoured with its unreliable Avia S-199s (nicknamed the 'Mule' for their terrible handling characteristics), the UN embargo against arms sales to the Middle East forced Israel to request more of the type from Czechoslovakia. No other country was prepared to supply fighter aircraft to Israel at the time. The Czechs responded by offering their now redundant Spitfires, a far superior aircraft. Of course the IAF was delighted to be offered a type that had always been right at the top of their shopping list and jumped at this opportunity.

At the time of the original Avia S-199 deal, a purchase of 25

surplus P-47D Thunderbolts from Mexico fell through as Israel was already committed to the Avias. One can only speculate on the impact a squadron or two of highly potent Thunderbolts would have had on the aerial balance of power in the region!

The Spitfires were assembled in Kunovice (now Let in Southern Moravia) and handed over to the Israelis to be either crated for shipping or modified for Operation Velveta.

The critical war situation in Israel meant that time was of the essence. The initial plan had been to disassemble and crate all the Spitfires to transport them by train to a Yugoslav port and then by sea to Israel, a time consuming exercise. Important military

23. George Lichter prepares to board Spitfire 2011 "White 26" at Podgorica, during Velveta 2, in December 1948. He was one the chief instructors and the examiner of the "Minus 1" and "Minus 2" pilot training courses in Czechoslovakia and held a similar post in Israel until late 1951. The Czechs are reported as being extremely impressed with his flying skills.
Of note is the CzAF applied eagle symbol to which the Israelis have added a Spitfire in the birds talons.
(IDF Archive)

campaigns were being planned by the Israeli High Command and they demanded a quicker solution.

Enter Sam Pomerance.

Sam Pomerance was not only a pilot but also an aircraft engineer. He suggested stripping all excess equipment from some of the planes, including guns and radios and fitting extra fuel tanks to fly them to Israel. This is where the idea of the 'Velveta' flights was born.

Pomerance took it upon himself to organise this work with the help of IAF technicians sent from Israel specifically for the task. He developed an improvised fuel pump system to cope with belly mounted slipper tanks, an extra internal tank replacing the radio equipment, plus Luftwaffe style 300 litre belly tanks mounted under each wing (a tank more usually seen on Luftwaffe Bf 109 & Fw 190 types and used by the Czechs on their Avia S-199s). Even with all of this extra fuel capacity, it was deemed prudent to have at least one refuelling stop between Kunovice and Israel. Although initially reluctant, the Yugoslavs finally agreed to allow the aircraft to refuel at Podgorica (also known as Titograd) in the south of their country near the Albanian border.

24. Dani Shapira (sitting on the nose) and Moti Fein, in front of one of their newly-acquired Spitfires at Podgorica during Velveta 2.

These two were among the first four Israeli pilots to get their 'wings' after going through the "Minus Two" course in Czechoslovakia. (native Israelis 'Tibi' Ben Shahar and Yeshayahu 'Shaya' Gazit were the other two) (Author)

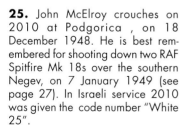

25. John McElroy crouches on 2010 at Podgorica , on 18 December 1948. He is best remembered for shooting down two RAF Spitfire Mk 18s over the southern Negev, on 7 January 1949 (see page 27). In Israeli service 2010 was given the code number "White 25".

'Virginia XII' was already on this aircraft when handed over to the Israelis at Kunovice. In all probability, it was a WWII RAF personal marking.

Can any reader confirm this? (IDF Archive)

Velveta 1, 24 - 27 September 1948

As soon as the first six Spitfires were prepared, Boris Senior, Modi Alon, Syd Cohen, Jack Cohen and Naftali "Tuxie" Blau were dispatched from Israel to Kunovice to ferry the aircraft home. The five pilots joined the team in Czechoslovakia and made final preparations for the mission. All those involved knew that the task they had taken on was important, perhaps crucial, to the survival of the new state of Israel.

The distance from Kunovice to Podgorica was a little under 500kms (300 miles) and, early on the morning of 24 September 1948, Sam Pomerance set out leading the six ship formation. The flight was uneventful until they arrived at Podgorica where 'Tuxi" Blau damaged his aircraft on landing. He made the classic landing error of forgetting to lower his undercarriage! Fortunately the Spitfire was not a write-off and was eventually freighted home in an IAF C-46 Commando. "Tuxi" was not badly injured and returned to Israel in the same C-46.

Three days later, on 27 September, the five surviving Spitfires took off for the 1100km (700 miles) flight to Israel. They were escorted by an IAF LATA (Air Transport Command - Lahak Tovala Avirit, in Hebrew) DC-4 transport that had arrived at Podgorica the previous day. It was equipped with dinghies and other rescue equipment in case any of the Spitfires had to ditch on the long over-water part of the journey. Additional escort was provided by a similarly equipped C-47, flown from an Israeli base to cover the final part of the journey.

Trouble struck within two hours of takeoff when, much to their consternation, Modi Alon and Boris Senior both discovered their fuel gauges were registering empty, their reserve fuel tanks having apparently malfunctioned. This necessitated an emergency landing at the nearest available airfield, the Greek Air Force base at Maritza in northern Rhodes. Both pilots were promptly arrested on suspicion of being Communists and their aircraft were impounded.

After finally convincing the Greeks of their bona-fides, Senior and Alon were released on 12 October. However both aircraft were retained by the Greeks, who subsequently crashed one killing the pilot. The remaining Spitfire was eventually returned to Israel in September 1950.

Sam Pomerance, with the two Cohens, arrived safely at Ramat David with D-132, 133 & 134, so that by the end of Velveta 1 a total of five Spitfires were available to the IAF. However, in October D-134 was destroyed in a crash, leaving just four until more could be flown in from Czechoslovakia. Though few in number, they still played a significant role in the war at that time.

D-132 became 2003 and D-133, 2004 under the IAF's revised numbering system introduced in November 1948.

26. The four Spitfires and their DC-4 escort ready to depart on the Yugoslavia to Israel leg of Velveta I. (Author)

27. The moment of departure from Yugoslavia. The Spitfire on the right is already taxiing. (Author)

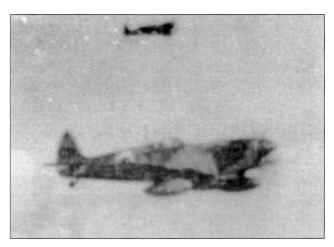

28 & 29. These two photos, taken 27 September 1948 on the Yugoslavia to Israel leg of Velveta 1, are rare in that they are some of the few known in-flight photos of IAF Spitfires with the German style underwing tanks and an RAF type slipper tank. (Author)

30. One of two Spitfires on Velveta 1 that fell into Greek hands. For some unknown reason the Greeks chose to write the pilots first name on Boris Senior's aircraft.

This photo was first published in Greece in the early 1950's. (Via Author)

Velveta 2, 18 - 26 December 1948

In the month following Velveta 1, a further fifteen Spitfires were tested and made ready for the long ferry flight to Israel. Twelve would eventually set out on the journey.

Operation Chorev (meaning Dryness), a fresh Israeli offensive in the southwest, was being planned for 19 December and the IDF General Staff considered it essential that more Spitfires be delivered before then. The Yugoslavs, however, were proving reluctant regarding the question of further flights over their territory and it was early December before they relented and permitted one last flight despite the UN embargo. Money changed hands.

For some obscure, possibly political reason, the Yugoslavs insisted that the aircraft be repainted in Yugoslav Air Force markings for the Kunovice to Podgorica leg. (refer Photo 31). On 18 December, after several days delay caused by severe winter storms, Sam Pomerance departed on the first stage of Velveta 2 leading an initial six Spitfires south from Kunovice. They were split into two, three aircraft sections with the first being Bill Pomerantz and Caesar Dangott flying with Sam Pomerance; and the second, John McElroy and Moti Fein led by George Lichter.

That day neither luck nor the weather were on the pilots side

and disaster struck when Sam Pomerance crashed and was killed during a snow storm in a mountainous part of Yugoslavia. Bill Pomerantz also lost contact with the others. George Lichter assumed command of the four remaining Spitfires and prudently made the decision to return to Czechoslovakia.

Back at Kunovice confirmation was received that Sam Pomerance was dead, a bitter blow to the ferry team. His remains were later recovered and buried in Israel. Some consolation, however, was Bill Pomerantz's survival. Engine trouble forced an emergency crash landing in Yugoslavia from which he escaped with only minor injuries. Frustrating for the mission though, his aircraft was a write-off. The two lost Spitfires were serial numbers 2006 and 2007.

The following day, 19 December, the persistent Lichter again set out with six aircraft divided into two sections. With him were Moti Fein and Dani Shapira as replacements for the two lost pilots. These two young men were only cadets on the "Minus 2" flying course run by Lichter & Dangott and were chosen because they were the best in their class.

31. Two Israeli technicians with former CzAF Spitfires, at Podgorica in December 1948 during Operation Velveta 2.

These three aircraft have the standard late WWII RAF colour scheme of *Dark Green* and *Ocean Grey* upper surfaces with *Medium Sea Grey* under surfaces. Note the hand painted Yugoslav national markings required for the flight from Kunovice. The number 632 on the nearest machine's fin relates to it's old CzAF serial SL632 and not to any 20XX serial in IAF service. At this stage the aircraft were unarmed and not fitted with radios which had been removed in order to fit an extra fuel tank behind the pilot. On the Velveta flights communication was by sight only. (IDF Archive)

32. Taken on the same day as Photo 34. Points of interest include the large four-digit serial on 2013 ("White 18" in 101 Sqn service) in the background. Sheer pressure of time and "different painters with different brushes" resulted in some Spitfires receiving these large "square" cornered serials while others were given small 10cm (4 inch) high serials under the tail. Note the incomplete national markings at the moment this photo was taken; plain white discs. (IDF Archive)

Both had logged minimal hours in Spitfires.

The second three were John McElroy (leading), Caesar Dangott and Arnold Ruch. Dangott was flying 2008, Fein 2009, Lichter 2010, Shapira 2011, McElroy 2012, and Ruch 2013.

At one point the inexperienced Shapira became disoriented in bad weather and had gone into a slow spiral. He was on the point of baling out when the calm and ever vigilant Lichter spotted him and was able to gain Shapira's attention. As the weather cleared all six made it safely into Podgorica, despite a fuel leak in Fein's aircraft which was repaired that night.

A second flight of six Spitfires left for Yugoslavia on 20 December: 2014, 2015, 2016, 2017, 2018 and 2019 piloted by George "Lee" Sinclair, Arnold Ruch, Alex "Sandy" Jacobs, Bill Schroeder, Aaron "Red" Finkel and Jack Cohen respectively.

Happily for Velveta 2's leaders, all twelve Spitfires had survived

33. Two technicians work on this Spitfire's Merlin engine. Note the SoD on the ammunition box 'seat'. (Author)

the first leg of the journey and between 21 and 26 December, preparations for the long over water flight home were made by technicians flown in from Israel. The part played by these men in the success of Operation Velveta cannot be over emphasised as it should be remembered that, like

the ex-CzAF Avia S-199's before them, these Spitfires were well worn and in need of reconditioning.

All Yugoslav markings were over-painted with Israeli national insignia during this period.

On 23 December four Spitfires, 2008, 2009, 2010 & 2011, piloted by Dangott, Lichter, Fein and Shapira respectively flew from Podgorica to Tel Nof in Israeli accompanied by IAF LATA C-46 1701. They completing the journey without incident, although it was found that Shapira's 2011 had a cracked engine block. Early on 26 December C-46 1702 left Israel for Podgorica and made the return trip later the same day escorting six more Spitfires; 2012, 2013, 2014, 2016, 2017 & 2018, piloted by; Sinclair, Ruch, Jacobs, Schroeder, Finkel and Jack Cohen. Fortunately this flight also went without incident. Near the coast of Israel Egyptian fighters could have been patrolling and so a Mustang of 101 Sqn rendezvoused with the unarmed Spitfires, escorting them for the last part of the journey.

34. Another photo in Podgorica on Velveta 2. These Spitfires have had their Yugoslav markings over-painted in white, in preparation for the addition of the dark blue stars in six positions. (IDF Archive)

Two machines which could not be made serviceable in Yugoslavia (2015 and 2019) were disassembled and transported to Israel in two C-46 Commandos of 106 Sqn two days later. With them went some of the huge quantity of spares and non-airworthy Spitfire airframe sections also purchased from the Czechs.

As with Velveta 1, the Velveta 2 aircraft had been extensively modified to enable maximum possible range. This delayed their entry into service while each aircraft spent several days having its military equipment refitted. However, at least four of them served during Operation Chorev and were involved in clashes with the RAF. As in all other phases of the Israeli Spitfire story the role played by ground crew and technical staff was equally as important as that of the pilots.

35. Another view of the Velveta 1 Spitfires and their improvised underwing tank installation. (via Author)

36. Caesar (pronounced Kaiser) Dangott on Spitfire 2008 at Podgorica during Velveta 2 in December 1948. Earlier he had been one of the two Chief Instructors of the "Minus Two" course in Czechoslovakia that trained the first four IAF pilots.
This photo gives a clear view of the improvised underwing tanks which were painted the grey-green colour of Israel's S-199s. Note the long cannon stubs fitted to training Spitfires by the CzAF. (IDF Archive)

SPITFIRE OPERATIONS
DURING OPERATIONS YOAV & CHOREV

Operation Yoav - 15 to 27 October 1948

Prior to a final peace settlement with its Arab opponents, the Israeli Government obviously desired that Egyptian forces be pushed back to the UN mandated international borders.

The first offensive designed to achieve this was Operation Yoav, unofficially nicknamed "Ten Plagues". Its military purpose was to force the Egyptian army out of the Israeli Negev and relieve the besieged settlements there. The offensive was timed to coincide with the earliest date sufficient ammunition and supplies would be available. In addition, by the middle of October the Galilee and Jerusalem fronts would be stable enough to allow a large transfer of troops to the Negev.

Spitfire D-130 was tasked with photo-reconnaissance in the lead-up to Yoav and the other four Spitfires were prepared for ground attack and air superiority work as well as could be done with the limited resources on hand.

On the offensive's first day, 15 October, only three of the four Spitfire *fighters* were available, D-132, D-133 and D-134, as D-131 was not serviceable. Their primary function was to support army operations in concert with the IAF's S-199s, Beaufighters and B-17 Flying Fortresses.

On the second day the three Spitfires from Herzliyya along with two 103 Sqn Beaufighters were assigned to hit Al Arish. Surprise was achieved on the first bombing run and all the aircraft came back to strafe the line-up of REAF aircraft. The Israelis claimed four

37. Chief of Defence Staff, Lieutenant General Yuakov Dori, speaks with Sandy Jacobs sitting in the cockpit of 2019 "White 19" at Hatzor Jan/Feb 1949. (Author)

38. Hundreds of citizens followed the funeral procession of Modi Alon. His casket was carried through the streets of Tel Aviv by 101 Sqn pilots with a Military Police escort. (Author)

Spitfires, either destroyed or damaged, and a large hangar hit, while the Egyptians insisted that only two aircraft were damaged by one of the bombs. REAF Spitfires finally scrambled but did not catch the IAF attackers before they returned to base. One of the Beaufighters suffered engine damage and was forced to divert to Tel Nof. Sadly, for the IAF, 16 October ended in tragedy. Modi Alon, 101 Sqn's charismatic Commander, flying S-199, D-114, was hit by AA fire and wounded over Majdal. Attempting to land back at Herzliyya he crashed and was killed. Syd Cohen took over as 101 Squadron leader.

The following day, 17 October, a number of Spitfire ground support missions had been planned, but a lack of serviceable aircraft foiled that idea, with just a single Spitfire sortie being flown, to escort three 69 Sqn B-17s bombing Egyptian artillery at Faluja.

Two Spitfires, including D-133 flown by Jack Doyle making his first flight for 101 Sqn, escorted a B-17 on a bombing mission over the Gaza Strip on the 19th. Major damage was inflicted and with the capture of Huleiqat the following day, which opened the road to the Negev, Operation Yoav began to wind down. The Army had achieved some of it's goals.

However, the campaign did not end so successfully for the IAF which lost Canadian Len Fitchett, his navigator Dov Sugerman and Stanley Andrews with their Beaufighter D-171 when it crashed behind enemy lines. They had been hit by ground fire while attacking the fort at Iraq al Suweidan. All three died.

While the General Staff took stock of the situation, the IAF was still in action on 20 October harassing Egyptian retreats. The army captured Beersheba on the 21st. That morning, Rudy Augarten and Jack Doyle, flying D-131 and D-132, were patrolling the area between Beersheba and Al Arish when they engaged four REAF Spitfires, claiming one destroyed each and a further one damaged.

39 & 40. Aaron "Red" Finkel, wearing his red baseball cap, surveys Spitfire 2004 "White 14" (formerly D-133) after a landing accident on 5 January 1949. The aircraft was damaged when a tyre blew out and the resulting nose-over wrote off the Spitfire. Finkel was lucky to escape only slightly injured.

This aircraft was one of the three Velveta 1 Spitfires and has the 101 Sqn badge on the port nose, underwing white/blue/white ID stripes (none on upper wings) and it's serial in hand painted 10cm (4 inch) high black digits under the tailplane. Note the bomb racks, severe light grey exhaust staining and remains of the temporary Yugoslav fuselage roundel showing as an off colour border around the SoD. (Lou Lenart)

SPITFIRE - Star of Israel

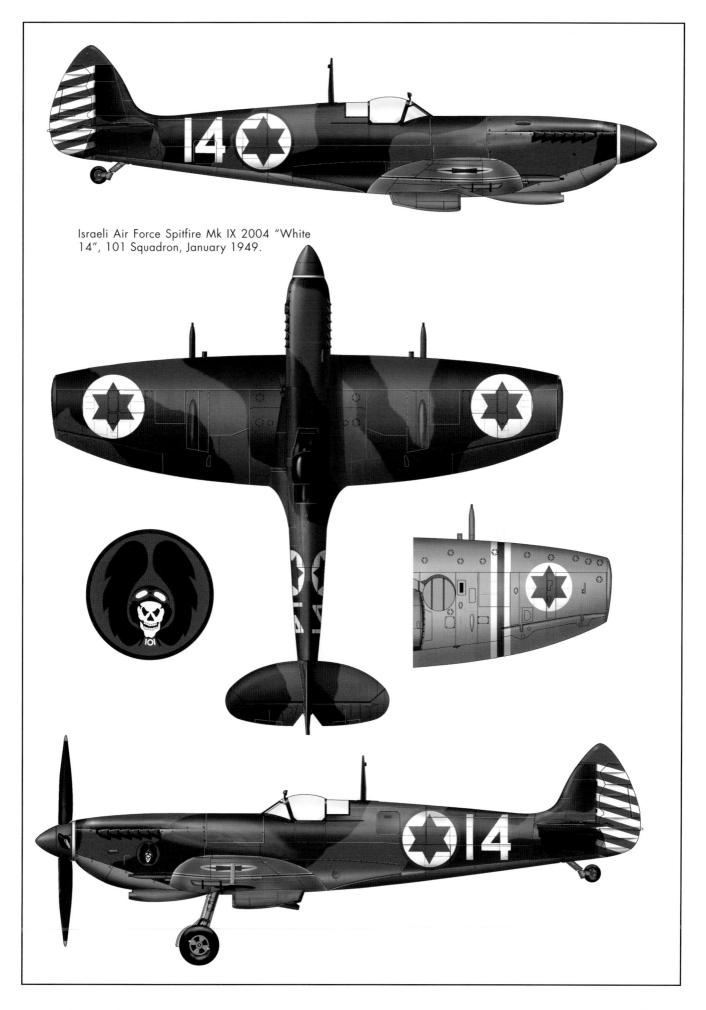

Israeli Air Force Spitfire Mk IX 2004 "White 14", 101 Squadron, January 1949.

Operation Chorev
22 December 1948 - 7 January 1949

Although there had been considerable success, the ultimate objective of Operation Yoav, forcing the Egyptians completely out of the Negev, had not been achieved. The General Staff planned a second campaign, Operation Chorev, to achieve this.

In the period between Yoav and Chorev the IAF improved its aircraft designation system by adopting a new four digit serial system. All Spitfires were renumbered in the 20XX series. For example, D-130 became 2001.

Extra Spitfires were on their way from Czechoslovakia and the IAF would add these to the four survivors (2001-2004), the six flyable S-199s and the first two P-51D Mustangs smuggled from

the United States. The Velveta 2 Spitfires arrived in Israel late in December (four on the 23rd and six on the 26th) and some were made operational in time to participate in Chorev.

As in Yoav, the Spitfire's main task was to perform ground attack missions, act as fighter escorts to the motley bomber force and maintain air superiority. Israeli Intelligence believed that the REAF had a five-to-one advantage in fighters. Fortunately for Israel, the UN embargo was affecting the Arab side in the conflict as much as them and the REAF proved to have less than a dozen each of Spitfire Mk IXs and MC.205Vs operational.

The first Spitfire sortie of Operation Chorev, on 22 December 1948, also brought the first IAF aerial victory of the new offensive when Rudy Augarten, once again paired with Jack Doyle (flying 2004), shot down one of the REAF's new Macchi MC.205V fighters over Al Arish. The pilot, Flt Lt Shalabi al Hinnawi, was badly injured but survived.

On the 27th two IAF Spitfires from Hatzor, including one piloted by "Buck" Feldman, were scrambled to intercept Egyptian fighters over the Al Arish area. Feldman was bounced by an MC.205V and his aircraft suffered minor damage.

The following day Gordon Levett flew his first Spitfire mission with 101 Sqn following his transfer from 106 Sqn, which operated C-47s. With him was 101 Sqn's Commander, Syd Cohen and their orders were to support the Army along the Khan Younis-Rafah front. The pair each carried two 250lb bombs, but neither managed to hit a train they spotted and attacked. A follow-up strafing with cannon and machine gun fire was successful.

The same day both Levett and Doyle were in action escorting four 35 Sqn Harvards on a bombing mission over Faluja. Six REAF Spitfires and two MC.205Vs were intercepted. The ensuing dog-fight saw Doyle destroy a Macchi, killing the pilot, Plt Off Ibrahim Nur al Din Abd al Fatah Sa'id; while Levett claimed the second MC.205V along with a 'probable' Spitfire. Also on 29 December a major tragedy was narrowly averted when Jack Doyle, leading two Spitfires, started to attack what he believed to be an Egyptian vehicle convoy. The pilots were not aware that the Israeli Army Negev Brigade were in the area and the two pilots broke off their attack only after a strafing pass which killed one soldier and wounded another.

Heavy ground fighting continued in the Faluja pocket and on 29 December Denny Wilson and Arnie Ruch escorted two 69 Sqn B-17s carrying out a raid there. After seeing the bombers safely out of the danger zone the two Spitfires headed for Al Arish where they tangled with

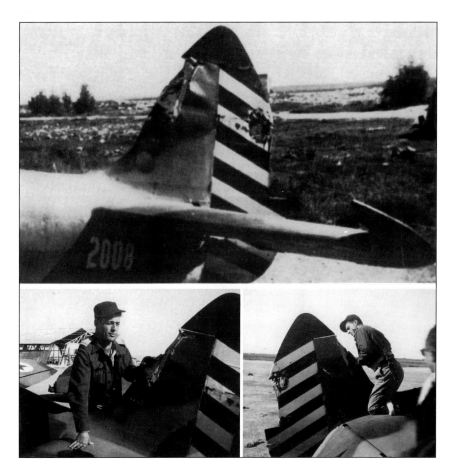

43 a, b & c. John McElroy examines the damage to Spitfire 2008 "white 15" caused by debris from one of the two RAF Spitfires he shot down on 7 January 1949. It was also slightly damaged in combat with REAF MC.205Vs on 27 December 1948, being flown by "Buck" Feldman on that occasion. (Arnie Ruch)

41, 42 (facing page) **& 44.** 2018 "White 17" & 2013 "White 18" from Hatzor providing fighter cover for two 69 Squadron ("Flying Hammers") B-17Gs which operated from Ramat David, on a bombing mission over the Faluja pocket.   By this time, January 1949, the IAF had gained air superiority over the battle zone.

Both Spitfires are in RAF/Czech *Dark Green & Ocean Grey* upper surfaces with *Medium Sea Grey* under surface camouflage scheme. Both have red & white 101 Squadron markings and "A" style radio numbers. Being Velveta 2 aircraft, neither have the 101 Sqn badge and both have underwing bomb racks. Note how faded the red spinner on "White 17" is.

B-17G 1602 (Photo 44 above) has the famous 'Mickey Mouse' scheme with a large cartoon on both sides of the fin. Note that the standard WWII tail gun mounting is missing and in its place is a Czech 7.62 MG - the same type of weapon was also installed in the waist positions.

Complete information, including four-view camouflage drawings and never before published photos of the Mickey Mouse cartoon on the starboard fin of this aircraft will be provided in our forthcoming Israeli B-17 monograph. (Author 41 & 42, IDF Archive 44)

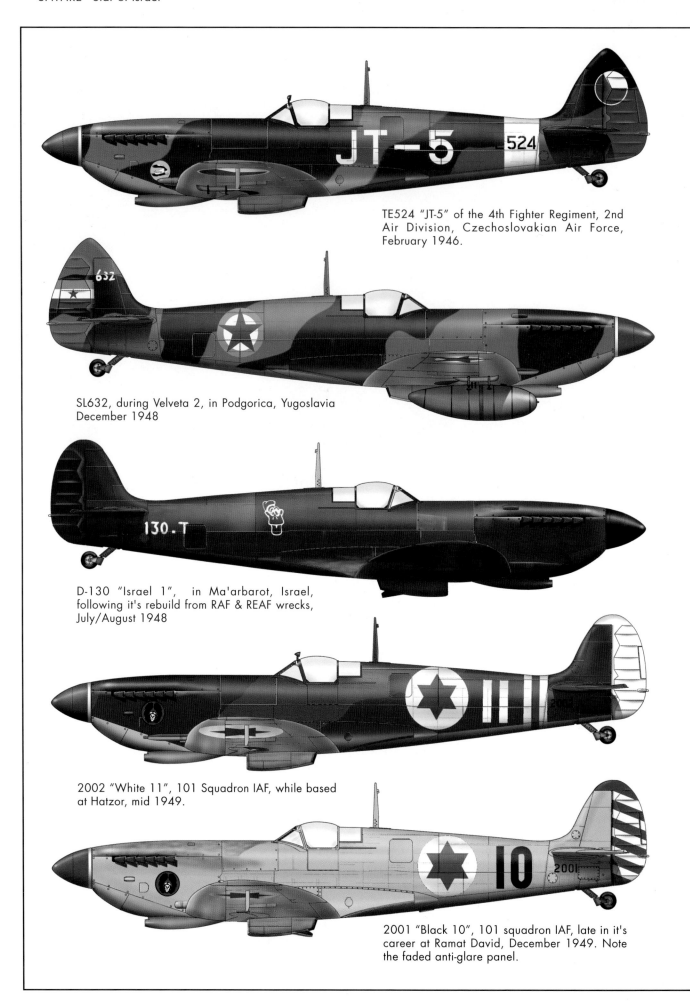

TE524 "JT-5" of the 4th Fighter Regiment, 2nd Air Division, Czechoslovakian Air Force, February 1946.

SL632, during Velveta 2, in Podgorica, Yugoslavia December 1948

D-130 "Israel 1", in Ma'arbarot, Israel, following it's rebuild from RAF & REAF wrecks, July/August 1948

2002 "White 11", 101 Squadron IAF, while based at Hatzor, mid 1949.

2001 "Black 10", 101 squadron IAF, late in it's career at Ramat David, December 1949. Note the faded anti-glare panel.

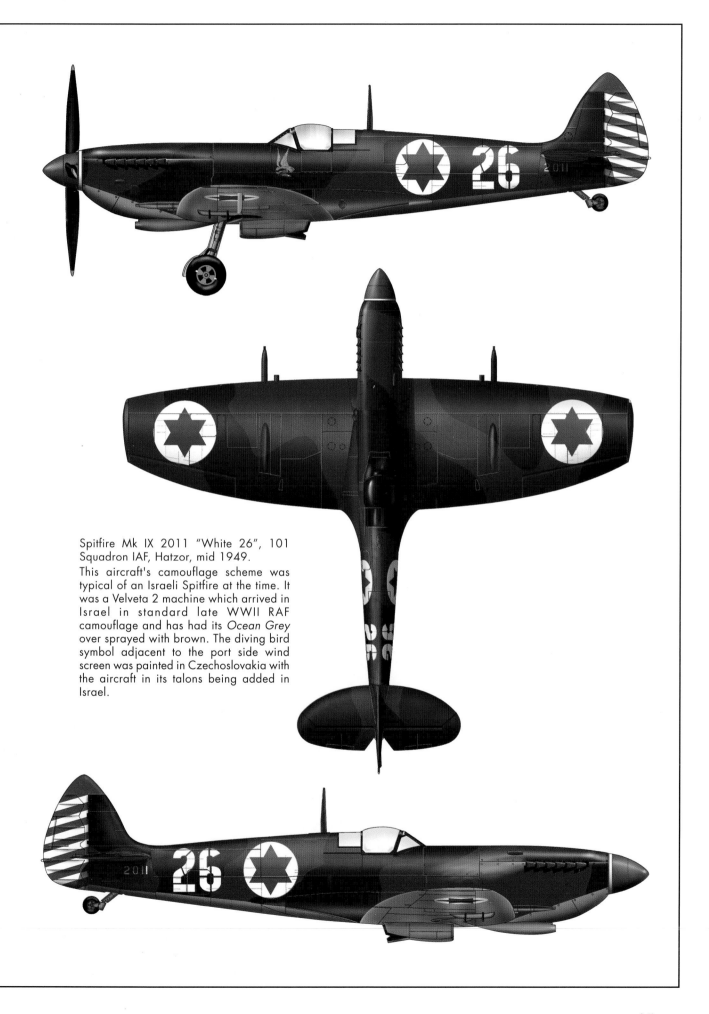

Spitfire Mk IX 2011 "White 26", 101 Squadron IAF, Hatzor, mid 1949.

This aircraft's camouflage scheme was typical of an Israeli Spitfire at the time. It was a Velveta 2 machine which arrived in Israel in standard late WWII RAF camouflage and has had its *Ocean Grey* over sprayed with brown. The diving bird symbol adjacent to the port side wind screen was painted in Czechoslovakia with the aircraft in its talons being added in Israel.

two REAF Spitfires, damaging both of them before heading home.

That same day a party of Israel's Harael Brigade, led by Yitzak Rabin (the youngest General in the Israeli Army at that time and Israeli Prime Minister 1992-95) raided one of Al Arish's satellite landing grounds. They secured two REAF Spitfire Mk IXs (including 664 "L") which were promptly trucked back to Tel Aviv / Ma'arbarot. The REAF was forced to hastily evacuate all its aircraft from its main Al Arish base.

Supporting the Army again on 30 December, Jack Doyle and John McElroy shot down two MC.205Vs (one each) that were strafing Israeli ground forces involved in fighting near the REAF's Bir Hama air base. Both pilots, Sqn Ldr Mustafa Kamal Abd al Wahib and Flt Lt Kahlil Jamal al Din al Arusi, were killed.

December 31 1948 saw Syd Cohen and Denny Wilson back in action over Bir Hama when Wilson spotted an MC.205V in its landing circuit and promptly shot it down (the pilot baled out and survived). During their return to base they intercepted an REAF Spitfire escorting a C-46 Commando and, using only his .5 inch Brownings to conserve scarce 20 mm cannon ammunition, Wilson shot the Spitfire down (this pilot also survived). To end an exhausting mission they joined two other 101 Sqn Spitfires and strafed an Egyptian Army truck convoy, destroying an uncounted number of vehicles.

On 5 January 1949 "Red" Finkel crashed Spitfire 2004 "White 14"

(refer page 20) while landing at Hatzor, when a tyre blew out causing the aircraft to flip on its back. Finkel's pride was injured more than his body, but the Spitfire was subsequently written off. That same day Rudy Augarten thought his luck was in when he strafed a line of aircraft at the small Bir Masaid landing strip which included REAF Spitfires, only to find that they were all dummy aircraft! To continue a busy day for 101 Squadron, Buck Feldman and Boris Senior, in a Spitfire and Mustang respectively tackled three REAF fighters over Al Arish, shooting one down and claiming a 'probable' second.

Operation Chorev and the War of Independence came to an end on the 7 January 1948 with the signing of final cease fire documents. The IAF had achieved complete command of it's own air space. Before the ceasefire came into effect at 4pm, Boris Senior & Jack Doyle, both flying P-51D Mustangs, and Arnie Ruch & Denny Wilson, both flying Spitfires, were involved in the last IAF versus REAF fighter combat of the War when they engaged eight REAF fighters above the Al Auja-Rafah road. The result was one Macchi MC.205V shot down by Boris Senior and damage to Wilson's wing.

One final act of the war remained to be played out - an engagement between RAF fighters and Israeli Spitfires.

28. 101 Sqn's Spitfire 2008 "White 15" being recovered after it crashed at Ramat David in July 1949. On 31 December 1948 Denny Wilson shot down an REAF Macchi MC.205V over the Faluja Gap in northern Sinai flying "White 15".
It's camouflage scheme is *Dark Green* and *Ocean Grey* upper surfaces with *Medium Sea Grey* lower Surfaces. (Yuda Borowick)

CLASHING WITH THE RAF

7 January 1949

From the beginning of the War of Independence the RAF had been conducting photo reconnaissance flights over Israel with impunity. Mosquito PR 34s of 13 Sqn, based at RAF Fayid in the Canal Zone, had been conducting the flights several times a week, much to the displeasure of the Israelis who suspected that the information gained was going straight to the Egyptians. Attempts were made to intercept these flights (including Spitfire D-131 on 22 October 1948) but the height at which the Mosquitos flew was too great for existing IAF aircraft.

The smuggling into Israel of the first P-51D Mustangs instantly remedied this deficiency and Mosquito VL625 was shot down by Wayne Peake flying Mustang D-190 on November 20. The RAF "took the hint" and Mosquito flights ceased for the time being.

By the last week of Operation Chorev the IAF had achieved almost total air superiority extending beyond Israel's borders and the Egyptian Government requested urgent help from the British. Assistance was provided by allowing retreating REAF aircraft to use RAF bases in Egypt with the unstated "safe haven" status they enjoyed. Also, political pressure was applied on Israel to withdraw to the international border. In the meantime, additional Spitfire FR Mk 18s of 208 Sqn and Tempest Mk 6s of 213 Sqn were transferred from Cyprus to Egypt to bolster the RAF presence in the area.

RAF Reconnaissance flights then recommenced and continued until ceasefire day, 7 January 1949, in order to monitor the Israeli withdrawal to their border. On that morning four 208 Sqn FR 18 Spitfires led by Flying Officer Geoff Cooper in TP340, together with Flying Officer Tim McElhaw in TP456, Pilot Officer Ron Sayers in TZ228 and Pilot Officer Frank Close in TP387, were

46. 2012 "White 16" after a winter downpour at Hatzor in Jan/Feb 1949. Colour scheme is *Ocean Grey* and *Dark Green* upper surfaces with *Medium Sea Grey* under surfaces and 101 Sqn colours on nose and rudder. The "A"-style radio code number is smaller than usual. This aircraft was piloted by 'Slick' Goodlin in the 7 January 1949 'incident' when he shot down RAF Spitfire Mk 18 TP340. (Author)

sent to patrol the Al Auja-Rafah road and monitor any fighting in that area. Prior to their arrival four REAF 2 Sqn Spitfires had attacked an Israeli armoured column near Rafah. Attracted by the smoke the four RAF Spitfires flew towards the area with both Cooper and Close peeling off for a low level pass over the column. It was not surprising that the Israelis reacted by defending themselves against 'another attack' and both RAF fighters were shot at. Close's engine was damaged forcing him to bail out. He landed badly, breaking his jaw, and was captured by Israeli troops.

Two IAF Spitfires, piloted by "Slick" Goodlin and John McElroy, were on patrol in the same area and were attracted by all the radio chatter that Close's shooting down generated. The RAF pilots had no idea that they might be attacked, while the Israelis regarded the RAF fighters as legitimate targets. From their perspective, the RAF fighters were over-flying a battle area and were automatically regarded as hostile. McElroy shot down Sayers' aircraft, killing him, and then promptly dispatched McElhaw who was able to bale out and, like Close, was captured. Debris from McElhaw's Spitfire damaged McElroy's propeller and tail section (photos 43 a, b & c).

Fg Off Cooper, in the last surviving RAF Spitfire, was engaged by "Slick" Goodlin who, after a lengthy dog-fight, was able to use the better manoeuvrability of his Mk IX to get into a firing position and hit Coopers' engine. He baled out and, despite a leg injury, was able to evade capture to eventually make his way home. McElhaw and Close were detained by the Israelis until late February 1949 when they were deporting by ship to Cyprus (photo 51).

Evidently none of the four pilots had radioed their plight back to Fayid. However, by early afternoon it became obvious to the RAF that something had happened to this flight of Spitfires. Therefore 6 Squadron based at Fayid and 213 Squadron at Deversoir were requested to

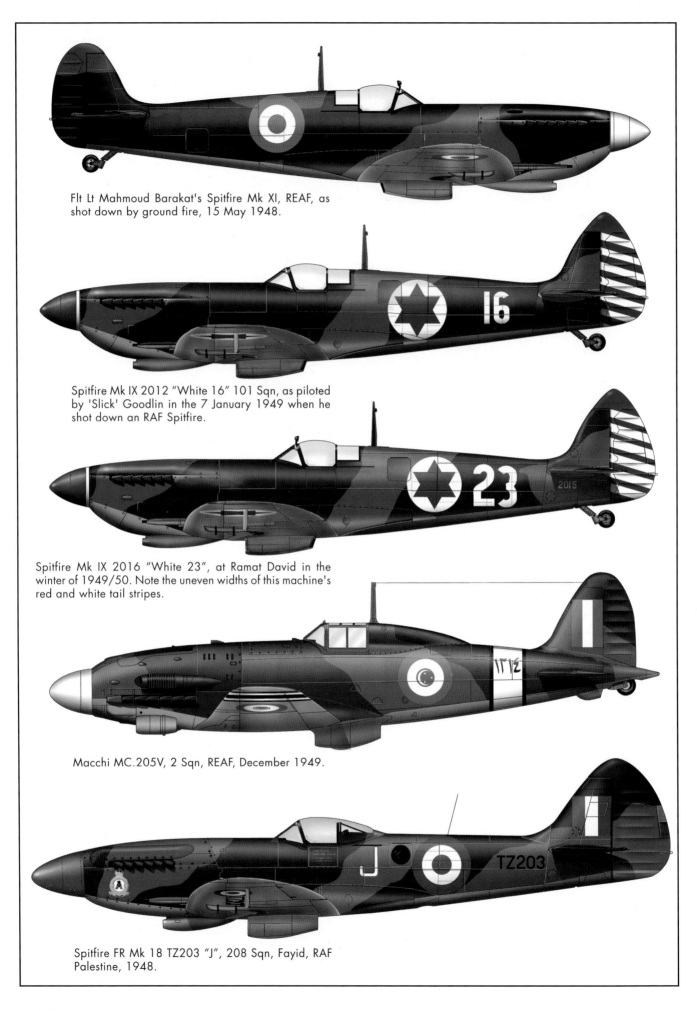

Flt Lt Mahmoud Barakat's Spitfire Mk XI, REAF, as shot down by ground fire, 15 May 1948.

Spitfire Mk IX 2012 "White 16" 101 Sqn, as piloted by 'Slick' Goodlin in the 7 January 1949 when he shot down an RAF Spitfire.

Spitfire Mk IX 2016 "White 23", at Ramat David in the winter of 1949/50. Note the uneven widths of this machine's red and white tail stripes.

Macchi MC.205V, 2 Sqn, REAF, December 1949.

Spitfire FR Mk 18 TZ203 "J", 208 Sqn, Fayid, RAF Palestine, 1948.

supply Tempests (eight from 6 Sqn and seven from 213 Sqn) to provide cover for four further 208 Sqn FR18 Spitfires while they searched for their missing comrades. The nineteen RAF fighters rendezvoused over Fayid and then headed for the search area, totally ignorant of what had happened or what they could expect from the IAF.

The IAF was mounting continuous patrols over the battle area and were expecting retaliation from the RAF. When four 101 Sqn Spitfire Mk IXs, piloted by Ezer Weizman, Sandy Jacobs, Casaer Dangott and Bill "Sure Shot" Schroeder spotted the RAF formation below them, they immediately attacked. Bill Schroeder, living up to his USN nickname, manoeuvred in behind 213 Sqn Tempest Mk 6 NX207 and shot it down, killing the pilot, Pilot Officer David Tattersfield. Weizman, in the meantime, managed to inflict damage on

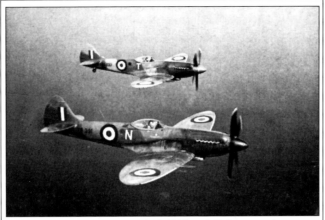

47. 208 Sqn's TP391 "White N" flying with TZ233 "White T" in late 1948. (Author)

another Tempest, NX134 'JV-T' of 6 Sqn flown by Pilot Officer Douglas Liquorish, and, in turn, received minor bullet damage from Tempest Mk 6 NX135 'JV-V' of 6 Sqn piloted by Flight Lieutenant Brian Spragg DFC.

At this point the Israelis broke off and returned home. There were no celebrations by the victorious pilots, just the general feeling that they "did what had to be done".

On returning to base several of the Tempests were found to

have bullet damage (quite severe in Liquorish's case), a testimony to the brief but violent battle they had experienced. During the clash some of the Tempests had confused the red-nosed IAF Spitfires with 208 Sqn Spitfires which also had red spinners. As a result, 208 Sqn immediately repainted their spinners white and added a white band to the rear fuselage. The following day the IAF went on a high state of alert as retaliation by the RAF, especially against the Spitfire base at Hatzor, was anticipated. Much to their surprise, nothing happened.

Interestingly, 208 Squadron's official history makes no mention of this 'incident' and it was twenty years before secret British documents were published that showed that the British government covered up all information regarding the loss of these aircraft and indeed the 'incident' itself.

Before the 'Incident'

Before re-equipping with Spitfire Mk 18's 208 Squadron flew Mk IX's. Some of these were left behind in Palestine as wrecks and were subsequently scavenged for parts by the IAF.

48. "RG-E" PV117 a green & grey camouflaged Mk IX operated by 208 Sqn in 1945. (MAP)

49. 'RG-S' ML401, 1947. Colour scheme is aluminium paint with black codes, anti-glare panel and serial with a red spinner. ML401 was struck off charge on 26 June 1947, while some other ex-208 Sqn aircraft continued to serve elsewhere.
For example, 'RG-Q' PV119 was transferred to the REAF on 30 April 1947 and 'RG-R' MH772 followed it on 27 November that year.
Egypt sold 'RG-Q' to Greece on 27 May 1948, while 'RG-R' was struck off charge the same day. (MAP)

A variety of reasons were offered by the RAF pilots to explain how such losses occurred - drop-tanks that wouldn't drop, guns that were not cocked, inexperienced pilots, bad weather conditions, etc. - but the main reason lay in the poor planning and guidance given to the squadrons involved by the RAF Command. The RAF failed to properly brief its squadrons on the full political situation as regards to the war between the Arab countries and Israel. It was an accurate reflection of the RAF's attitude towards the IAF that they believed they could over-fly both Israel and battlefield areas and not expect the IAF to react.

As an interesting postscript to this 'incident'; one year later an RAF Sunderland which was flying from its base in Aden, on the Persian Gulf, to Egypt, flew over Ramat David. Two Spitfires from 101 Sqn intercepted it and signalled the flying-boat crew to land off Tel Aviv. These instructions were ignored until one of the Spitfires fired warning shots. The crew were brought ashore and, much to the Israelis amazement ,they discovered that the navigator's maps still showed

50. Tempest pilot David Tattersfield was given a military funeral in Israel. Here six IAF military policemen in full ceremonial uniform guard his coffin which is draped in wreaths and the Union Jack. (Author)

51. Flying Officer Tim McElhaw, who was shot down by the IAF on 7 January was deported to Cyprus in February 1949. Here he is escorted by an IAF officer and an official of the Israeli Ministry of Foreign Affairs. The sign above the door reads, "The Israeli Marine Police Haifa Port". (Author)

Israel as British controlled Palestine. The entire crew were not aware that the State of Israel even existed.

52. TZ233 "White T", a Spitfire FR Mk 18 of 208 Squadron RAF having its guns serviced at Fayid in late 1948. It is in the standard RAF camouflage scheme of *Dark Green* and *Ocean Grey* upper surfaces with *Medium Sea Grey* lower surfaces. It has 208 Sqn's red spinner and D-type roundels. The Squadron's spinners were quickly changed to white after the clash with IAF Spitfires on 7 January 1949. (Author)

EGYPTIAN SPITFIRES

While Spitfires of the Royal Egyptian Air Force are beyond the scope of this book, those which fell into Israeli hands are covered on the following five pages.

Captured airframes were a welcome source of spares to keep the IAF's own Spitfires flying, with engines and guns being the most highly prized items.

53. An REAF Spitfire attacking an Israeli column on the road to Rafah. (Author)

54. A line-up of REAF Mk Vb Spitfires at Kasfaret Air Base in the Nile Delta, May 1947. Colour scheme was RAF *Dark Earth* and *Mid Stone* upper surfaces with *Azure Blue* lower surfaces, white spinner & fuselage code letter with black/white/black rear fuselage ID bands.

Aircraft 'C' in the foreground was serialed 'ER602' on it's white section of the ID band (Arabic number on top and English underneath). It appears that 'ER602' was not it's original RAF serial because that number was allocated to a machine which was destroyed in an anti-aircraft artillery friendly-fire accident on 21 December 1942.

It was an REAF Mk Vb (serial ER610) that Modi Alon shot down, flying an S-199, over Majdal on 15 July 1948. (Author)

55 & 56. IAF technicians strip Spitfire Mk IX '622', 2 Squadron REAF, after it crash-landed near Majdal on 5 November 1948. Engine failure seems the most likely cause of the crash, as there were no IAF combat claims against REAF Spitfires that day.

The pilot, Flt Lt Mustafa Kamal Nasr, survived the crash and managed to avoid capture and safely return to Egyptian territory. (Govt. Press Archive)

Spitfire 664

The Israeli Army captured this 2 Squadron Royal Egyptian Air Force Spitfire Mk IX serial 664, intact but unserviceable, on 29 September 1948.

The aircraft was in RAF *Dark Earth* and *Mid Stone* upper surfaces with *Azure Blue* lower surfaces and black & white identification striping on the wing-tips and rear fuselage. The serial number appears in Arabic only. Its individual code letter is 'L' but this appears only on the starboard fuselage, possible in red.

As a general rule, REAF policy regarding Spitfires was to have the full style of roundel on the fuselage only, while wing roundels were plain with no crescent or stars in their centre.

57. 664 at an Al Arish air base satellite field, prior to being dismantled and trucked back to Tel Aviv. Fourth from the right, among some of his troops, is Yitzhak Rabin who was to become the Chief of Staff during the 1967 war and later Prime Minister of Israel, 1992-1995. (Govt. Press Archive)

58. IAF technicians readying 664 for transportation. Note the call sign letter 'L' is just visible between the arms of the person standing forward of the fuselage ID band. (Govt. Press Archive)

59. 664 with wings removed, tied down ready for departure. (Israeli Air Force Magazine)

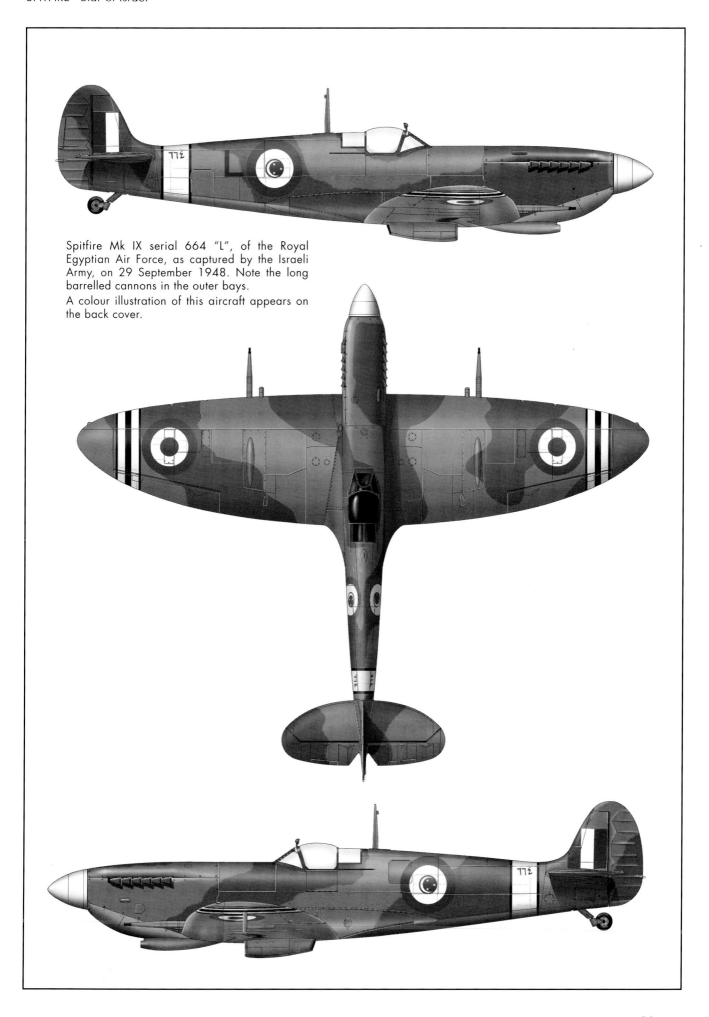

Spitfire Mk IX serial 664 "L", of the Royal
Egyptian Air Force, as captured by the Israeli
Army, on 29 September 1948. Note the long
barrelled cannons in the outer bays.

A colour illustration of this aircraft appears on
the back cover.

63. A captured REAF Spitfire bought to Ma'arbarot, July/August 1948. A North American Harvard centre section is in the background. (Author)

64. A shot down Egyptian Spitfire Mk IX wreck, stripped of all useful parts and abandoned. (Author)

65. This Spitfire was recovered from Bir Hama, an emergency satellite air strip near Al Arish.
The serial of this machine is not known, however it is definitely not 664. (Author)

Egyptian or Not ?

60, 61 & 62. On the 15th of May 1948, one day after the start of hostilities, this REAF Mk IX Spitfire was shot down by Israeli ground fire at Sde Dov, sparking off a controversy that persists to this day. (Govt. Press Archive)

In 'Spitfires Over Israel', by Brian Cull, Shlomo Aloni & Dr David Nicolle, published by Grub Street, it is stated that there is still a good deal of doubt as to the origins of this Spitfire. The REAF have always strenuously denied that this was one of their aircraft and stated that the pilot, Flight Lieutenant Mahmoud Barakat, was not known to them.[1]

The author has interviewed two witnesses to this incident, one who saw the crash and inspected the aircraft close-up and the other who sat in on the pilot's interrogation after capture.

Amnon Yogev was a ten year old boy when he saw this aircraft being recovered from the beach. He distinctly remembers its green & grey camouflage and the green & white national markings. The photos here show no sign of the crescent moon and three stars that are normally present on REAF roundels of the period. At that time, the REAF was revising it's standard regulations for the design and placement of roundels, serials and codes so numerous variations occurred. For example 664 (see page 33) has a code letter "L" on the starboard fuselage but not on the port side, while 622 (see photos 55 & 56) carried only the Arabic serial number, and no code letter.

The lack of completed roundels or ID striping and no serial number simply indicates that Barakat's aircraft was in the process of having full markings applied when it was rushed into service at the start of hostilities.

The second witness was Lou Lenart (S-199 pilot) who was present at Flt Lt Barakat's interrogation. He related to the author that the Egyptian showed him a photo of his wife and two year old daughter, one of his two children. It transpired that Flt Lt Barakat was the son of the Chief of the Cairo Cavalry Police, had been the Special Assistant to the Under Secretary for Air in Cairo and his pilot training was with the RAF at Ismailia. He was eventually returned to Egypt during an exchange of P.O.Ws after the final ceasefire.

The above aircraft most certainly did belong to the REAF and Flt Lt Barakat was an REAF pilot. The only controversy in Israel surrounding this incident is not the identity of the aircraft and pilot, but exactly who was responsible for the shooting down, an AA battery or rifle fire.

Editors note...
[1] In later correspondence with the publisher Dr Nicolle indicates his revised opinion that this Spitfire was Egyptian.

AFTER THE WAR...

A pictorial essay

66. This is the flight line at Ramat David air base in August/September 1949, just after 101 Sqn transferred there from Hatzor. A variety of types are in evidence including:- two P-51D Mustangs, Spitfire "Black 10", one of the IAF's three Beech Bonanzas, a Spitfire still with a large 4-digit serial number on the rear fuselage and another under construction. Note the main service hangar to the right and a revetment with a large 'NO SMOKING' sign on the wall, painted when the RAF operated from this base. (IDF Archive)

67. Spitfire Mk IX 2016 "White 23", at Ramat David in the winter of 1949/50.
As with "White 26" (See page 40), this is a rare example of the small four digit serial appearing in white under the tailplane. Colour scheme is still RAF *Ocean Grey* and *Dark Green* upper surfaces with *Medium Sea Grey* under surfaces. Note the unusual proportions of 2016's red and white 101 Squadron rudder stripes.
A colour illustration of this aircraft appears on page 28. (Yuda Borowick)

68. Pilots volunteered from around the world to fight for Israel, including former Royal Canadian Air Force pilot Lee Sinclair.

Taken during the War of Independence, this photo of Lee Sinclair's aircraft is unique, in that it is the only one known of a Spitfire in service in 1948, excluding Operation Velveta, where a slipper tank was carried.

The author has studied Operational Training Unit (OTU) students log books and established that these tanks were sometimes used in later years on long training flights. For example Ari Aloef flew 2015 "White 23" on 105 Squadron's second operational training course (OTU 2). He flew a sortie from Ramat David via Alat and Haifa then home to Ramat David non-stop, on 26 January 1951, with a slipper tank fitted. (Lou Lenart)

69. Another Canadian, Jack Doyle, was the most successful IAF fighter pilot in the War of Independence.

He already had two Luftwaffe kills in WWII and added a further four in Israel - two REAF MC.205s and two Spitfire Mk IXs. He returned to Canada after the War. (Lou Lenart)

70. A good view of the German designed 300 litre drop-tanks (more usually seen on Bf 109s & Fw 190s!) on an Israeli Spitfire Mk IX at Hatzor in 1949. The stencil under the wing reads "LOCATION FOR WING-TIP STEADYING TRESTLE" in 1" capitals, unchanged since the aircraft rolled off the Supermarine production line! Note the carburettor intake cover has been removed. (IDF Archive)

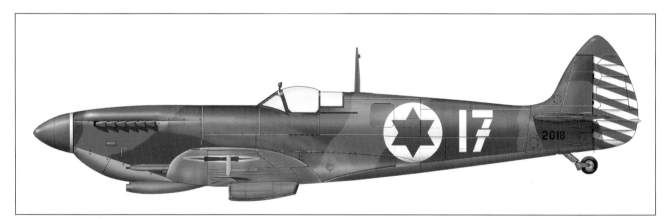

71. Looking rather weather-beaten, 101 Squadron's Spitfire 2018 "White 17" sits in the sun at Hatzor in mid 1949. Colour scheme is *Dark Green* and brown upper surfaces with *Medium Sea Grey* under surfaces. This aircraft is illustrated in the side view above. (Yuda Borowick)

72. Ladya Shiyovitz, a Czech Jew who was recruited directly into the "Minus One" Flying Course in Czechoslovakia.

He was later killed, just weeks before the 1956 war, performing a barrel roll in an Dassault Ouragan jet when his engine cut out, causing the aircraft to crash.

The Hebrew woman's name "Shoula", on this unidentified Spitfire, is red with black shading and above the name is a reclining nude woman. Personal markings, on IAF aircraft of this period, were exceedingly rare and the author would welcome more information on this particular aircraft.

73 & 74. (also see photo **1**) In mid 1949 a detachment of 101 Squadron aircraft were dispatched to Azion air strip north of the Negev for an adverse weather exercise (to test maintenance procedures for their aircraft in difficult climatic conditions). From the heavy coating of dust and sand in these photos, they certainly chose an ideal location! The aircraft in Photos 1 & 74 is 2003 "White 12" and the pilot is Dani Shapira, who eventually flew more than 100 aircraft types and was the sixth person to cross the Mach 2 barrier. He achieved this feat in an early Mirage while testing the type in France. Crouching on the ground, in photo 1, is fellow pilot Grisha Braun.

Note the pattern of the *Dark Green* and hand painted brown camouflage on this machine. At the time the IAF had no standardised camouflage pattern, each painter simply made up his own when orders were received to over-paint the original *Ocean Grey* with brown. "White 12"'s serial number was the 30cm high black style as per 2025 in photo 53. The fuselage Star of David is also further forward than usual. (73 Author, 74 Dani Shapira)

75. Spitfire Mk IX 2011 "White 26", of 101 Squadron at Hatzor in mid 1949. (Author)

76. Dani Shapira stands next to the CzAF applied symbol that was retained on this aircraft in Israeli service. This was the actual Spitfire that he flew to Israel on Velveta 2.
The Spitfire clutched in the eagle's talons was added by IAF staff. No doubt it represents an Egyptian Mk IX. Code numbers are the thick stencilled "A" style, associated with Ramat David in later years. All the other markings are standard. (Author)

77 & 78. What a difference a few months make!

These two photos of "White 26" were taken later in 1949, shortly before 101 Squadron shifted to Ramat David. In just a few months the paint finish has weathered to such an extent that the old Czech fuselage codes "MP" are starting to show through.

"MP" designated the 5th Fighter Regiment, 2nd Air Division and was previously 312 (Czech) Sqn RAF which used the codes "DU" during WWII.

Of interest is that the panel with the bird symbol appears to be a slightly different colour to the surrounding area. (IDF Archive)

78. Pilot Eli Feingash is 'signing' for "White 26" with Chief Technician, Yehuda Pelpel. See page 25 for a three view colour illustration of this aircraft. (IDF Archive)

79. Spitfire Mk IX's 2014 "White 24" & 2002 "White 11" at Hatzor in 1949. Note the white/blue/white fuselage ID bands still present on "White 11" together with it's original out-sized fuselage national insignia applied in 1948. In mid 1949 the IAF was not in the habit of repainting it's aircraft unless they really needed it! (IDF Archive)

80. Spitfire Mk IX's and personnel of 101 Squadron awaiting inspection at Ramat David in late 1949/ early 1950. (Author)

81. Activity on the flight line at Ramat David on 10 September 1949. Spitfire "White 31" is a good example of the radio code number being painted directly over the serial. 2025, in the background, is undergoing final assembly and was yet to receive its radio code number. Generally at Ramat David the two large white "A" style radio code numbers were painted directly over the black serial numbers. A colour illustration of "White 31" appears on the back cover. (Author)

82. Spitfire "White 18", warming up at Hatzor, March 1949. This aircraft was from the Velveta 2 batch. (Author)

36. Another picture of "White 18", here warming up in a revetment at Hatzor in June 1949, just prior to 101 Squadron's shift to Ramat David.
Note the starter cable leading away from the starboard nose socket. (Author)

84. A line-up of twelve 101 Squadron Spitfires at Ramat David in late 1949. The fuselage Star of David on "White 33" is much further aft than usual which has resulted in the radio number being pushed back almost to the tailplane. As usual, the radio number has been painted directly over the serial number, partially obscuring it. Behind "White 33" is 2024 with its SoD in the usual position. (Author)

Israeli Spitfire Mk IX Variants

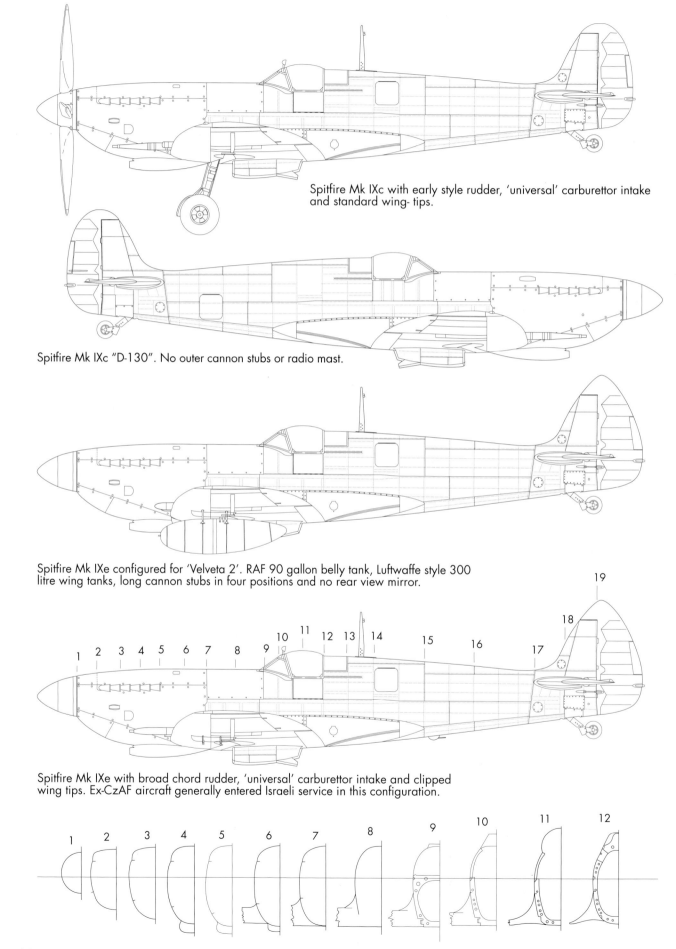

Spitfire Mk IXc with early style rudder, 'universal' carburettor intake and standard wing- tips.

Spitfire Mk IXc "D-130". No outer cannon stubs or radio mast.

Spitfire Mk IXe configured for 'Velveta 2'. RAF 90 gallon belly tank, Luftwaffe style 300 litre wing tanks, long cannon stubs in four positions and no rear view mirror.

Spitfire Mk IXe with broad chord rudder, 'universal' carburettor intake and clipped wing tips. Ex-CzAF aircraft generally entered Israeli service in this configuration.

Plan views show a typical Mk IXc

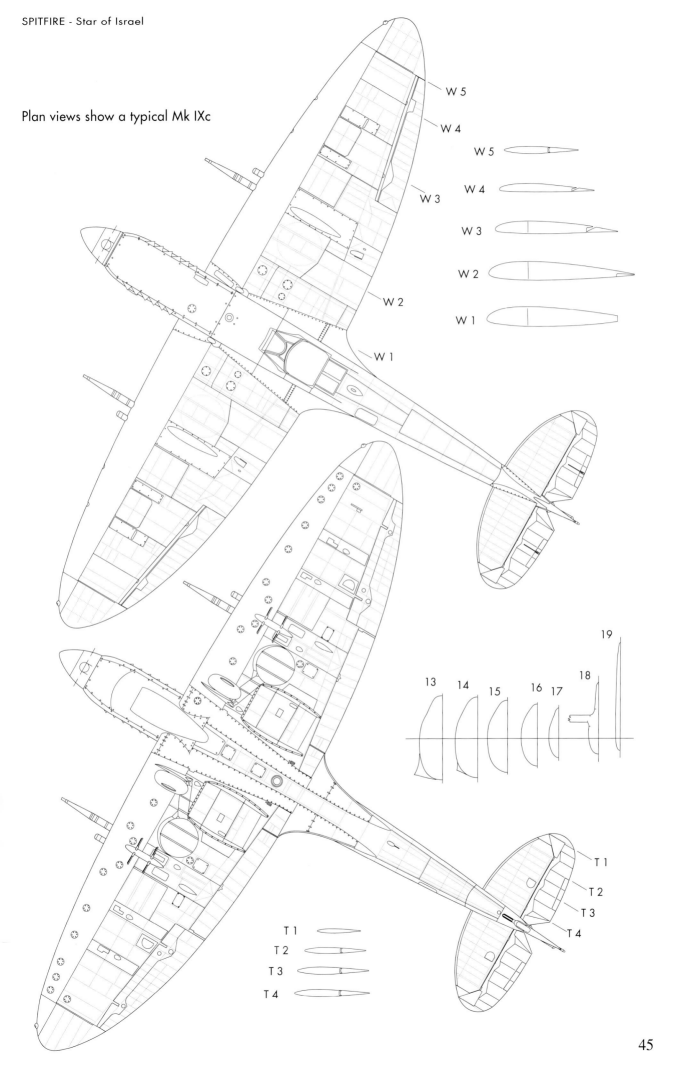

W 5
W 4
W 3
W 2
W 1

T 1
T 2
T 3
T 4

13 14 15 16 17 18 19

CAMOUFLAGE & MARKINGS 1948/49

Camouflage colours & tactical markings

Controversy has persisted down through the years regarding Israeli Air Force camouflage colours in 1948/49. The simple answer is that Israel was under great pressure to get newly acquired aircraft into service and standardising paint schemes was a low priority. Aircraft were used in whatever scheme they arrived in, or were painted in any paint available to achieve a brown & dull green upper surface with light blue under surfaces.

The author has interviewed several retired IAF technicians who laughed at the suggestion that any kind of standardised colour scheme existed during the 1948/49 period. According to them ground crews simply sprayed or hand brushed old RAF paint, paint purchased from Czechoslovakia as part of the Spitfire deal, or even resorted to house paint! To add to the confusion, machines in service were rarely repainted to comply with revised tactical markings applied to newly arrived aircraft.

For example, see photos 13 and 79. As late as mid 1949 "White 11" still wore the rear fuselage bands applied in September 1948, even though they had been superseded by underwing bands in October 1948, as applied to 2004 "White 14", then dropped altogether for aircraft entering service in December 1948.

From Improvisation to Standardisation

The Spitfires in this book entered service in **three distinct groups** and a progression from total improvisation to some semblance of standardisation is clearly evident.

The **first two Spitfires** D-130 & D-131 were assembled and tested in dark green primer and D-130 at least, had various white chalk cartons, mechanics names and 'D-130' roughly drawn on. By the time they were taken on charge by 101 squadron at Herzliyya both were painted dark green on most surfaces with hand painted "shields of David" applied in six positions. As with the earlier S-199s size and placement varied considerably. White/blue/white rear fuselage bands were added plus 20cm (8 inch) high black serials and the 101 Squadron badge on the port nose. (photo 6).

The final two stages of this evolution, for D-131, were a brown disruptive pattern added to the upper surface and later still, light blue under surfaces. D-130 was striped to bare metal to improve speed in its new Photo Reconnaissance role.

The second group were the three **Velveta 1 Spitfires**. They arrived wearing standard 1944 pattern RAF *Ocean Grey* and *Dark Green* upper surfaces with *Medium Sea Grey* undersurfaces. All three had red spinners with white backing plates, as applied in CzAF service, which 101 Squadron adopted as its own.

At the date of entering service the Velveta 1 Spitfires had black serial numbers, white, hand painted individual aircraft numbers, 101 Sqn badge and white/blue/white identification stripes painted under their wings. The Israeli Army had requested stripes under the wings rather than on the rear fuselage, as

per D-130 & D-131, to improve identification from the ground. Their national insignia in six positions was now to a smaller standard size compared to the rough hand painted markings of the two earlier aircraft.

The third group of Spitfires covered in this book, the **Velveta 2 Spitfires**, also arrived in standard RAF/CzAF camouflage and red spinners. These aircraft were never given white/blue/white fuselage or under wing identification stripes or the "Angel of Death" badge on the port nose. Only the first five Spitfires ever received the squadron badge.

Green and brown camouflage

After the incident with the RAF on 7 January 1948, the IAF High Command ordered 101 Squadron to replace the *Ocean Grey* portion of it's Spitfire's upper surface camouflage with brown for improved camouflage effect and to reduce confusion with RAF aircraft. This transition from grey/green to brown/green took some months and was achieved by simply brushing or over spraying the *Ocean Grey*.

Numbering Systems

On 31 May 1948 the IAF issued orders regarding it's first standardised national insignia and numbering systems.

A Hebrew letter was assigned to each class of aircraft: Light aircraft were given "Alet" (N), eg Piper Cubs and Austers; light bombers and small transports "Bet" (I), eg Norseman and Bonanza; B-17 heavy Bombers were assigned "Hay" (H); heavy transports "Samech" (V), eg DC-4, C-46 and C-47; fighters were assigned "Daled" (D) eg S-199

Stencil applied "A" type numbers

1234567890

Mosquito and Spitfire. Within the fighter category Spitfires were assigned the D-130 to D-159 range. These serial numbers were to be painted on the rear fuselage forward of the tailplane in 20cm high digits with 2cm stroke widths.

Also included in the 31 May orders were basic instructions as to the size and placement of national insignia. This comprised the 'Shield of David' on a white disk and was to be painted in six positions. As all aircraft in service with the IAF at that time were light aircraft, measurements for the white disk were specified at 85cm diameter above and below wings and 45cm for fuselage insignia.

Later in 1948, when the first S-199s and Spitfires entered service, these instructions were superseded in the field as required. Interestingly some S-199s still received the small 45cm fuselage insignia.

In mid November 1948 an improved system encompassing serial numbers for individual aircraft and radio calling code numbers was introduced. Each serial number was to consist of four digits with the first pair representing the aircraft type and the second pair the individual machine. It was to be painted under the tailplane. For fighter types 19 was assigned to S-199s, 20 to Spitfires, 21 to Mosquitos and 23 to Mustangs. Thus an aircraft serialed 2035 would be Spitfire number 35.

Serial number styles

When Spitfire D-130 & D-131 were taken on charge their black 20cm number was applied using the same stencils as had been used to number the S-199s.

The November 1948 "20XX" system saw three different styles of size and placement appear:

1) Stencil applied 'Squarer' numbers about 30cm high on the fuselage forward of the tailplane. This style was painted on Velveta 2 aircraft in Czechoslovakia or Yugoslavia (photo 32, Spitfire 2013). In the case of Czech Spitfires dismantled and freighted to Israel these 30cm high numbers were applied in Czechoslovakia (photo 81, Spitfire 2035). This style of number was still in evidence in the mid 1950's and was used on various types including Harvards and Stearmans at that time.

2) Small hand painted black numbers approximately 10cm (4 inches) high under the tailplane as in the case of the 2004 (page 20).

3) 15cm high white stencilled numbers as in the case of 2011 "White 26" (photo 75) and 2008 "White 15" (photo 43).

Radio code number styles

Call sign numbers were first applied in November 1948 before Operation Chorev, as 75cm high thick stroked white numbers. Apart from some rare examples such as "White 14" (page 21) and "White 16" (photo 47), these numbers were applied using a single

85. Compare the weathered surface of "Black 10" in this photo taken at Ramat David in 1950/51 with photo 12 on page 7. Modellers building Israeli aircraft of from this period should take particular note of their rapid surface deterioration. (Yuda Borowick)

set of hand cut sheet metal stencils which is still in existence today. In later years this actual set of stencils was associated with aircraft painted at Ramat David.

(throughout this book the author refers to these as "A" style numbers for convenience. This is not an official IAF designation)

They were used until the early 60's on Gloster Meteors, Dassault Ouragans and Sud-Ouest Vautours. Being hand made, the stencil set was not created to an exact mathematical formula which accounts for the lack of perfect symmetry in each digits design. Modellers take note! The actual stencil shapes, as traced for the author, are reproduced at the bottom of page 46.

Generally a Spitfires individual serial number would also become it's radio call sign. However for Velveta Spitfires this tended not to be so for two reasons.

Firstly: at the time, November 1948, 101 Squadron was a mixed formation of S-199s, Spitfires and Mustangs with the early single digit numbers taken up by the surviving S-199s. Hence D-130 became "10" and D-131, "11" etc.

Secondly: newly delivered Spitfires tended to enter service out of serial sequence, while squadron commanders gave their aircraft radio call signs based purely on the order in which they entered service.

Rudder stripes

Prior to Operation Yoav in late September/early October 1948 rudders on all fighters in service with 101 Squadron were given red and white diagonally stripped rudders, a permanent Squadron marking, as distinct from the earlier white/blue/white fuselage or underwing bands, which were intended only as temporary ground recognition markings. The application of the stripes varied slightly from aircraft to aircraft with an extreme example being 2016 "White 23" whose red stripes were much narrower than it's white ones (photo 67).

In later years the two other squadrons to operate Spitfires, 105 and 107, were assigned black & yellow and blue & white rudder stripes respectively.

The second part of "Spitfire - Star of Israel" completes the Israeli Spitfire service history and camouflage and markings evolution through to the mid 1950's. Part 2 will include colour chips mixed to original paint samples.

Extra details about some IAF personnel mentioned in this book:

Modi Alon...	ex-RAF fighter pilot and 101 Sqn Commander
Rudi Augarten...	ex-USAAF
Naftali "Tuxie" Blau...	ex-SAAF 1 Sqn fighter pilot who flew Spitfires in North Africa
Grisha Braun...	an Soviet Air Force Yak pilot in WWII
Joe Cohen...	ex-Indian AF pilot. He was killed in late 1950 when he crashed his Spitfire at Ramat David - he had been doing a barrel-roll to celebrate his promotion to Major
Syd Cohen...	ex-SAAF fighter pilot. He took over 101 Sqn when Alon was killed
Jack Cohen...	ex-SAAF 4 Sqn fighter pilot
Caesar Dangott... IAF's	US Navy in the Pacific pilot who became one of the two Chief Instructors in the "Minus 2" flying course
Sam Feldman...	ex-USAAF pilot
Eli Feingash...	a native Israeli
Alex "Sandy" Jacobs...	a Palestine-born ex-RAF pilot
John McElroy...	249 Sqn RAF & 421 Sqn RCAF in WWII with nine kills, awarded the DFC & Bar
Moti Fein...	one of the first native Israeli pilots
Seymour "Buck" Feldman...	former RAF Tempest pilot with 9.5 V1 kills, awarded the DFC
Aaron "Red" Finkel...	ex-USAAF
George Lichter...	ex-USAAF 487 FG fighter pilot with two kills and Instructor of the IAF cadet pilots at Kunovice
Gordon Levett...	RAF pilot in WWII and published author regarding his IAF experiences
Maurice Mann...	ex-RAF pilot
Bill Pomerantz...	ex-USAAF 318 FS fighter pilot with four kills
Arnold Ruch...	ex-SAAF 40 Sqn pilot
Bill "Sure Shot" Schroeder...	former US Navy pilot
Boris Senior...	ex-SAAF
Dani Shapira...	one of the IAF's first four pilots
George "Lee" Sinclair...	a Canadian former Wing Commander in the RAF
Nathan Suffin...	ex-RAF
Ezer Weisman...	current President of Israel
Denny Wilson...	ex-RCAF 411 Sqn with two kills